D0555892

Extraordinary Projects from Ordinary Objects #1

THE LOOK • LEARN & DO SERIES™

Written and Illustrated by Mark Icanberry

Look • Learn & Do Publications

Extraordinary Projects from Ordinary Objects #1

Dear Parents and Educators,

Safety is always a primary concern with children's projects. This icon means that adult supervision or permission may be advisable for a particular step of the project.

Adult Supervision

Each project offers three versions. The level of difficulty is indicated by one of these symbols:

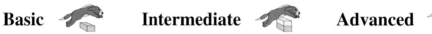

Basic   **Intermediate**   **Advanced**

We hope you and your children have fun with the projects in this book!

Sincerely,

The Look • Learn & Do Family

Extraordinary Projects from Ordinary Objects #1 © 2000 by Mark Icanberry
Created by Mark Icanberry
Illustrated by Mark Icanberry, Arthur Mount, and Jordan Romney
Layout by Carlton Rémy • Edited by Pennfield Jensen • Copy Edited by Pamela Evans

I dedicate this book to my son David. Special thanks to my friends and family, and most of all to my wife, Nina, for her incredible support, patience, and love.

ISBN 1-893327-04-3
Library of Congress Control Number: 00-192722
Printed in Singapore
10 9 8 7 6 5 4 3 2 1

Look • Learn & Do Publications
www.lldkids.com

Distributed by Ten Speed Press, P.O. Box 7123, Berkeley, CA 94707 • www.tenspeed.com

TABLE OF PROJECTS

Greenhouses   5–9
With water and light, your
plants will grow right!

Blimps   11–15
Amazing super-lifters and
around-the-house drifters!

  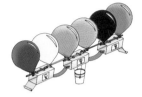

Bubble Blowers   17–21
Simple, easy, lots of fun,
bubbles are for everyone!

Birdbaths   23–27
Splish-splash. Birds have
fun in their bath!

Compasses   28–31
A needle, a magnet, a pen …
you'll never be lost again!

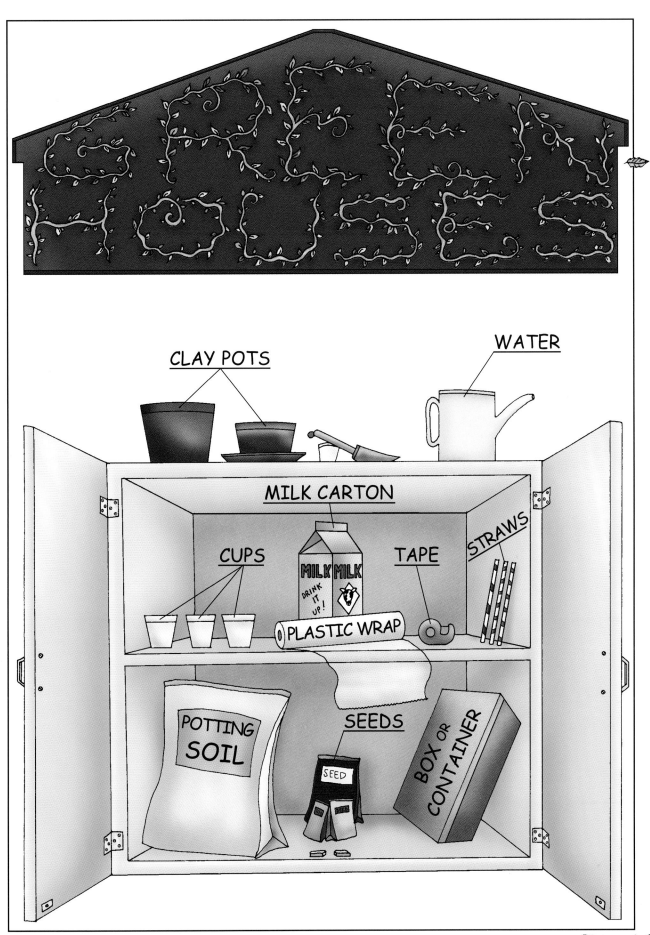

A greenhouse can be made from many different supplies, as long as the plants are in some kind of well-lit, enclosed environment.

Seeds

Any kind of seeds will do, but it's best to select seeds for plants that won't grow too big.

If you can't find any seeds around the house, sprouts are great; they grow fast and stay small, *and* you can eat 'em! You can also go outside and dig up a small plant or seedling to transplant. (Be sure to get permission before digging up plants in a garden!) If you do this, get as much of the roots as possible and keep the roots moist when you replant.

Clear Plastic

Clear plastic, such as plastic wrap or a plastic bag, is what you want. You could also use a dry cleaner's bag—check out the closet!

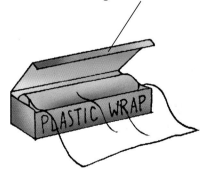

Tape

Clear tape works great for building your greenhouse. Any kind of tape will do, but clear tape lets in more light.

You don't have to use the exact supplies listed here, or build your greenhouse exactly like the ones shown on the next page.

If you want to make a bigger greenhouse, use a larger cardboard box. You could even use a wooden box, such as an orange crate. Remember, larger boxes will take up more room, so consider the amount of space you have and how many plants you want to grow.

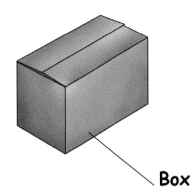

Box

Any cardboard box will work for the base of your greenhouse.

Cups

Many kinds of cups will work for growing plants in your greenhouse. A good choice would be plastic or Styrofoam disposable cups.

Milk Carton

Your best choice is a half-gallon milk carton, as it will hold several plants.

Straws

It is best to use the straight kinds of straws. If you only have the kind that bend, cut off the bent part.

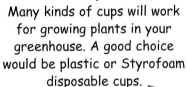

Soil

Potting soil works best, but you may also use dirt from outside.

Plants need good soil to grow healthy and strong. If you can, use potting soil, which can be found at any nursery or home improvement store. Otherwise, use dirt from outside. Make sure it's crumbly and doesn't have too many stones and twigs, so the roots will be able to spread out.

The Clear-Cup Growing Hut

This is one of the simplest projects in the whole book! You will need two clear plastic cups. Place some soil in one, and then add your seeds or small plant. Water the soil, and place the second clear plastic cup over the top. Put the clear-cup growing hut in a well-lit area, but it's best if it's not in direct sunlight all day long, as the heat could cook your plants. Make sure to keep the soil moist.

You can tape the two cups together.

Use a strip of cardboard taped to both ends of the box across the top to hold up the plastic, as shown.

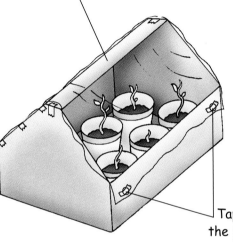

Tape pennies to front corners of the plastic to hold it down yet allow access for watering.

The Big Box Greenhouse

1) Cut a cardboard box into the shape of a house. I like to cut it at an angle up toward the middle (as shown) so it looks like a house with a glass roof.
2) Cut and tape the clear plastic over the top.
3) Place soil in your cups. If you are using seeds, follow the directions on the packet about how deep to plant them and how much to water them.

The Milk Carton Greenhouse

1) Cut a half-gallon milk carton in half, as shown.
2) Securely tape the ends of the straws to the corners of the carton, creating an A-frame shape. Tape the fifth straw across the top, as shown.
3) Carefully cut and tape plastic wrap on all sides of the straw roof frame, leaving the front section untaped so you can get inside your greenhouse.
4) Water your plants and place them inside your greenhouse.

Try using one long sheet of plastic that goes from the back of your greenhouse, across the top straw, and down the front.

Cut separate pieces of plastic for the ends of your greenhouse, and carefully tape them on.

Try planting sprouts. They grow fast and stay small, and best of all, you can eat 'em.

Small Plants

Instead of planting seeds in your greenhouse, you can use small plants that have already sprouted. Carefully scoop them out with an old spoon or something similar. Gather up as much of the root base as possible in your scoop. Transplant into the growing container, adding soil if you need to, and place in your greenhouse. Be sure to water immediately.

Once your greenhouse is complete, find a good spot for it. You will want one that has lots of natural light.

Keep in mind that too much direct sunlight could cook your plants rather than help them grow! Also, the more sunlight the plants receive, the more water they will need.

Watch Your Plants Grow

Make sure to water your plants regularly. You want to keep the soil moist. If your plants outgrow their greenhouse, you can replant them in bigger containers or outside. How about keeping a daily log of how much water you use and how much your plants grow?

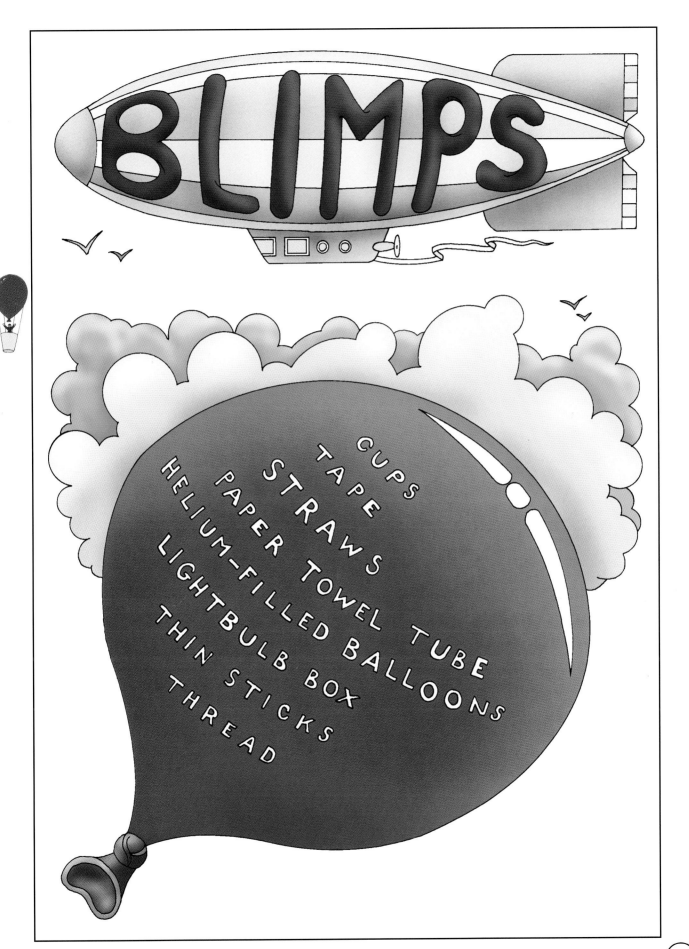

BLIMPS

CUPS
TAPE
STRAWS
PAPER TOWEL TUBE
HELIUM-FILLED BALLOONS
LIGHTBULB BOX
THIN STICKS
THREAD

For each of the blimp projects, you will need some helium-filled balloons. The rest is up to you and your imagination.

You'll have to buy some helium-filled balloons. You can find them at most flower shops, gift stores, and toy stores. You can also find small tanks of helium for sale at some of these locations, if you decide to fill up the balloons yourself. If you have trouble finding such tanks, look under "Helium" in the Yellow Pages of your telephone directory.

Straws

Straws are great because they are hollow and light.

Skewers

These can be used in place of straws. Be sure to get wooden ones (not metal), because they're lightweight.

Helium-Filled Balloons

These will help your blimp rise up into the air.

Thread

Sewing thread works well, but any lightweight twine or string will do the job.

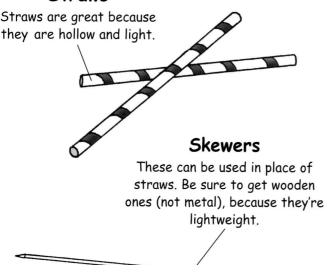

Experiment with different kinds of supplies. Keep in mind that more balloons are needed to lift heavier materials.

A gondola is a cabin suspended underneath an airship or blimp. You can use lots of different items to make the gondola for your blimp—the lighter the better. You can put various things inside your gondola to find the perfect float weight. (You can even use a milk carton for your gondola, but be sure to drink all the milk first. We recommend chocolate chip cookies with it!)

Containers
Many types of containers may be used for your gondola, including a lightbulb box, a milk carton, or a paper cup.

Cups
Small paper or Styrofoam cups are great because they are lightweight.

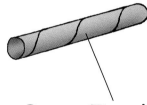

Paper Towel Tube
The tube from a roll of paper towels makes a perfect Torpedo Blimp gondola.

Tape
Any kind of tape will work, but clear tape is best because it weighs very little.

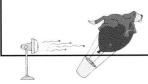

The Paper Cup Flyer: Simple to make, and it may fly higher!

Add one long string to act as a tether so you can pull your blimp back down from the ceiling.

1) Tape three or four pieces of thread to the sides of a paper or Styrofoam cup.
2) Tape or tie the other ends of the thread to the balloon.
3) If the balloon is not able to lift the cup, cut away the top of the cup to lighten it. Or add more balloons!

The Super-Lifter: With several balloons, this blimp really zooms!

The sky is the limit, so use your imagination and experiment with supplies. I tried all sorts of materials with the super-lifter, and they all worked fine.

The more balloons you use, the more lift your blimp will have.

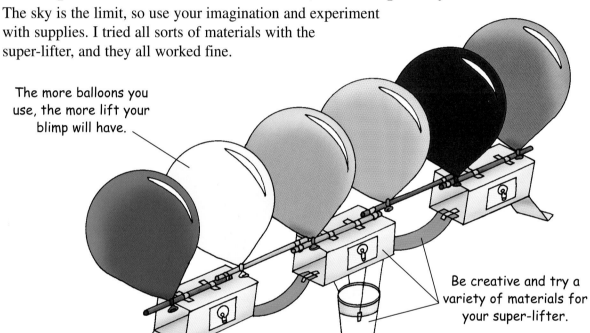

Be creative and try a variety of materials for your super-lifter.

The Torpedo Blimp could be made by a chimp!

1) Draw some doors and windows on a paper towel tube, which will be the gondola.
2) Tape two or three balloons to the paper towel tube.
3) Insert some small items in both ends for ballast (see next page), such as pennies or paper clips.

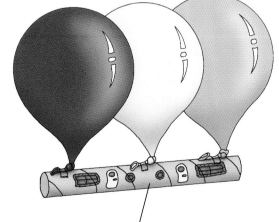

Tip: If you don't have a paper towel tube, you can tape two or more toilet paper tubes together.

Neutral Buoyancy

This can be a fun and challenging experiment. Have some pennies, paper clips, or small squares of paper ready to serve as ballast. (Ballast is anything that adds weight to your blimp to give it stability.) Add them one by one until your blimp reaches neutral buoyancy—which means that it's simply floating, going neither up nor down. Your balloons will begin to lose their helium rather quickly, and naturally this will affect the neutral buoyancy.

Once your blimp is complete and wants to float up, up, and away, slowly add small items to the blimp's gondola.

Shucks. David's shoe is too heavy. It won't float.

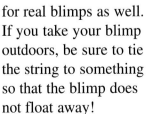

Experiment

Once you've completed your blimp and it has achieved neutral buoyancy, take the blimp to rooms or places with different temperatures. Try achieving neutral buoyancy next to the refrigerator, and then slowly open the refrigerator door and see what happens! Cold air or warm air should affect how it floats. This is true for real blimps as well. If you take your blimp outdoors, be sure to tie the string to something so that the blimp does not float away!

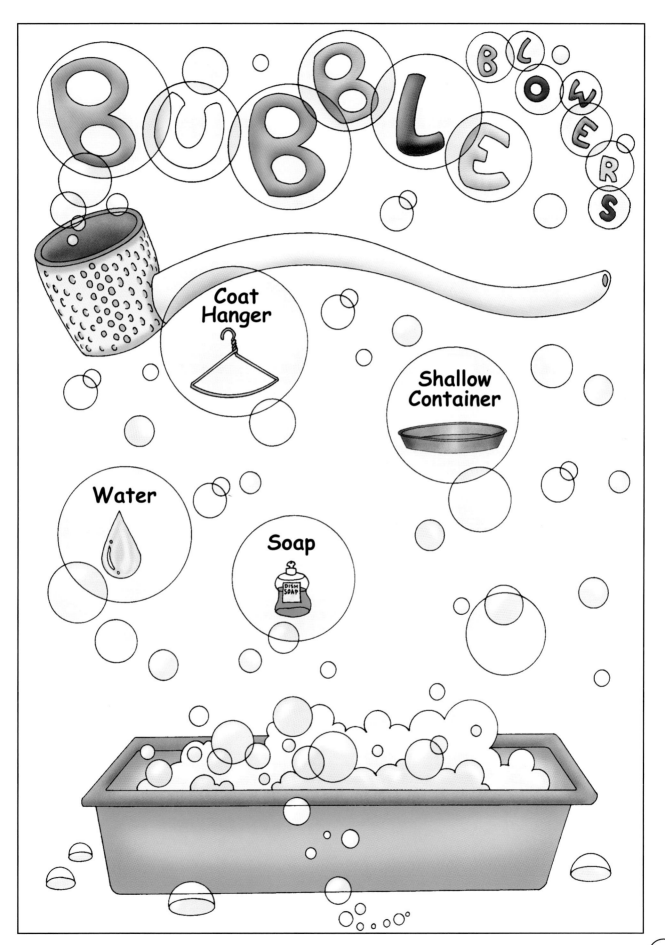

Bubble blower supplies are very simple: a wire coat hanger, dish soap, and a big shallow container like a pie pan or baking tray.

Shallow Container
Pie pans or baking trays are perfect because they are shallow and large enough to make big bubbles. The bigger the better! To make super bubbles, you could even use an upside-down garbage can lid. Or see how small you can make some bubbles with different stuff like straws.

LEMON DISH SOAP

Dish Soap
Dish soap works great and is easy to mix with water. However, you may use just about any kind of soap, including shampoo. (But remember, a little soap goes a long way!)

There are lots of different ways to make bubbles. Experiment with other kinds of supplies to see how many ways you can make them.

A Single Hoop to Swoop

1) Twist the wire so that it forms a hoop on one end. The bigger the hoop, the bigger the bubble will be.
2) Bend a smaller hoop on the other end and squash it to form a handle.
3) Remember, make your hoop no bigger than your soap tray.

Super-Hooper

1) Bend the wire so that it forms one big circle.
2) Bend two pieces of wire into U-shapes for handles. Twist these onto opposite sides of the circle.
3) Remember, make the bubble hoop no bigger than your soap tray. (I used a plastic garbage can lid turned upside down.)

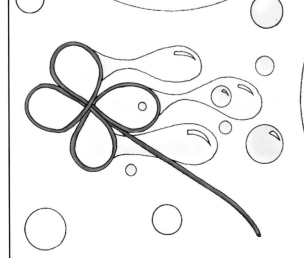

The Four-Leaf Clover Bubble Blower

1) Straighten out a wire coat hanger.
2) Bend the wire into four different circles, each one next to the other, as shown. Where the four circles meet, be sure all the pieces are touching the main stem. This will help ensure that each circle is independent of the others and will make its own bubble.
As always, experiment with your own ideas.

Bubble Solution

Making bubble solution is easy. Just put some warm water and a little soap into a container. Add only a small amount of soap at first, and test it to see how well it works. You could even keep notes on how much water and soap you mix together. For example, four cups of warm water to one tablespoon of soap makes a good bubble solution. Experiment with three or four different batches. Once you determine the best mix, you'll be able to make perfect bubbles every time.

I wonder what the bubbles would look like if I added food coloring to my bubble mix.

Blowing Bubbles

Tip: The slower you move your hoop through the air, or the slower you blow into the center of the hoop, the bigger your bubbles will be. There is almost no limit to the sizes you can create. See who can make the smallest bubbles! (Try a straw.) In the sunshine, you can watch all the colors of the rainbow dance on the surface of the bubbles.

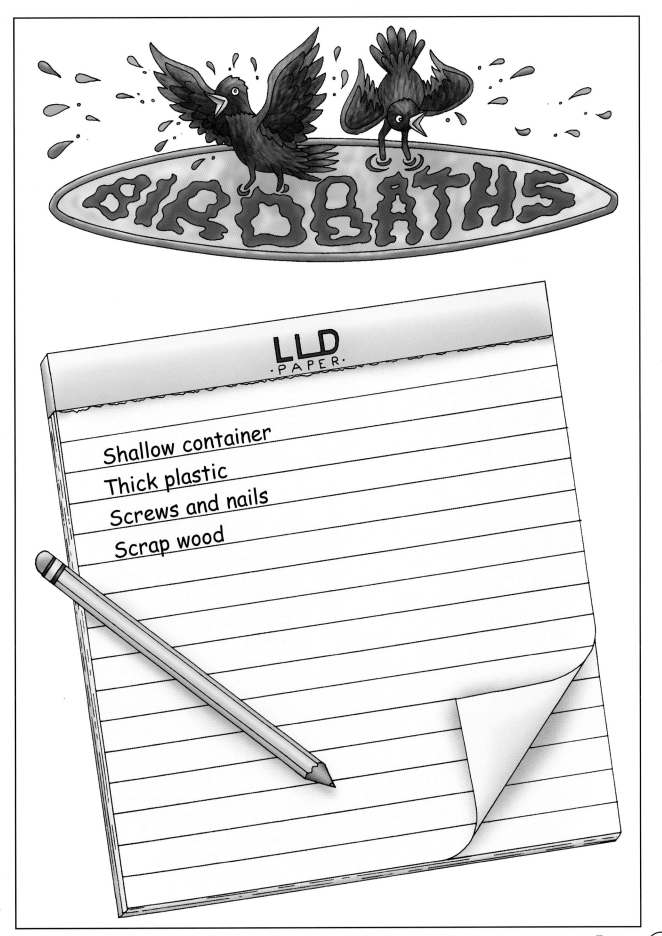

BIRDBATHS

LLD
·PAPER·

Shallow container
Thick plastic
Screws and nails
Scrap wood

For a basic birdbath, all you really need is something to hold water. A large clay plant pot bottom is perfect. It's heavy with low sides.

If a plant pot dish will hold water for a plant, it will work for a birdbath. In fact, it is one of the best things to use for a birdbath. It is heavy and has a wide rim that birds can rest on before and after bathing. You can buy one at the store. They're not very expensive, and best of all, they're meant to be outside.

Since we need this pie pan, I guess we'll just have to finish off the pie.

Clay Pot Bottom

A clay pot bottom works great for a birdbath, but any shallow container will work. Remember that whatever you use will be left outside.

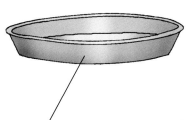

Pie Pan

A pie pan also works fine for a birdbath. Remember that it must be something that will not leak.

Thick Plastic

If you plan on building a pond for your birdbath, you will need a big piece of plastic. A full-size plastic garbage bag works well.

If you build a birdbath with a stand, keep in mind that you will also need some basic carpentry tools, like a hammer and saw.

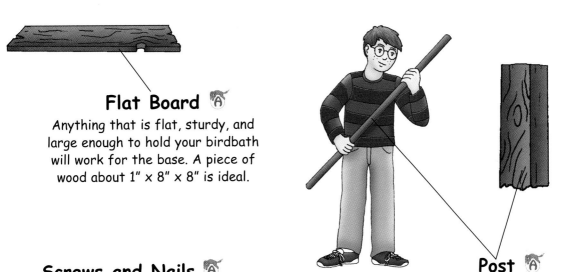

Flat Board
Anything that is flat, sturdy, and large enough to hold your birdbath will work for the base. A piece of wood about 1" x 8" x 8" is ideal.

Screws and Nails
If you are planning to build a birdbath stand, you will need screws or nails to put it together.

Post
A 4" x 4" piece of wood is perfect. You could also use an old broom handle or a shovel handle. (Just be sure the broom or shovel is no longer in use!)

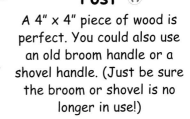

Scrap wood can be built into a birdbath stand. Just about any size will work for the flat base, as long as it is large enough to hold your birdbath.

Find a spot off the path for your Basic Birdbath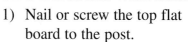

Simple, easy, and can be placed anywhere. The bigger the bath, the bigger the bird?

Just add water to your container, and voila!

Once you've completed your birdbath stand, simply place the pie pan (or whatever you are using as your birdbath) on top of it. Add water.

Tip: Such a stand also works well for a bird feeder.

Birds love to land on a Birdbath with Stand

1) Nail or screw the top flat board to the post.
2) Find a good spot for your birdbath (remember, it's permanent), out of the way but in full view for watching the birds.
3) Dig a hole deep enough to securely hold the stand firmly upright (at least a foot into the ground, and not much wider than the post).
4) After placing the post in the ground, pack the dirt around it so it won't wobble.

Fill with water—but not too deep. An inch is plenty.

Tip: This is also a nice spot to test a small boat.

Birds will be fond of your Bird Bathing Pond

1) Most important, find a good place for your bird-bathing pond (see next page).
2) Dig a hole about one inch deep and slightly smaller than your piece of plastic. Use the dirt you dug up to make a small berm (a raised ridge) around the edge of the pond.
3) Lay in the plastic and cut off any excess.
4) Put rocks around the outer edge to hold the plastic in place.

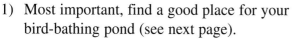

Select a good spot for your birdbath . . . one that will attract birds and allow you to observe without disturbing them.

A Strong and Sturdy Stand

There are lots of ways to make a stand for your birdbath. Scrap lumber works great. It is important that the stand be sturdy so it won't fall over. Make sure that the top is securely fastened to the post and that the post is anchored solidly in the ground.

Concern for the Environment

Leaving plastic in the ground is harmful to the earth and its animals. If you make a bird bathing pond, be sure to remove the plastic if you decide not to have a birdbath anymore.

Tip: If you have a bird feeder, you might want to put your birdbath nearby. Birds will be happy—they can dine *and* bathe!

Just add water, and presto, a birdbath! Remember, birds won't use it if the water is too deep. An inch or less is fine.

Location! Location! Location!

Be sure to select a good place for your birdbath or bird pond. You don't want it where people walk, where other animals play, or too close to a building—or else birds won't use it.

Who said you were a bird, Newton?

Please be sure to select a spot that is not frequented by cats!

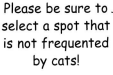

COMPASSES

This is possibly the hardest project in this book. Be patient and try to follow the directions carefully. And experiment with your compass!

You will need a magnet to make a compass. (Otherwise you'll get lost!) Almost every refrigerator has a magnet stuck on it somewhere. But if yours doesn't, you might want to ask a neighbor to check their refrigerator for you.

Magnet

You have to have one to magnetize your needle.

Cup

A clear plastic cup is best because you can see what's going on inside of it.

Cork

A piece of cork works great when making a floating compass. If you can't find a cork, try using a bottle cap or anything small that floats.

Pencil

If you are planning on building a hanging compass, you will need a pencil or pen.

Needle

A pin or sewing needle is perfect. The larger it is, the more it can be magnetized.

Hanging Compass

1) Use a marker to write N, S, E, W on the cup.
2) Magnetize your needle (see next page).
3) Tie one end of a short piece of thin thread to the center of your magnetized needle.
4) Attach the other end of the thread to a pencil.
5) Place the pencil across the rim of a plastic cup, allowing the needle to hang freely inside the cup. The needle should be pointing north.

The balance has to be just right, or the leaf will tip over.

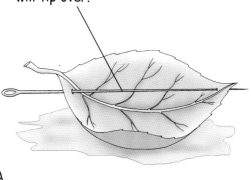

Camping Compass

1) Find the perfect leaf—one that is curved like a boat.
2) Magnetize your needle (see next page).
3) Carefully lay or insert your magnetized needle in the center of the leaf.
4) Place your camping compass on very still water. If balanced just right, the needle will point north.

Tip: Be sure to keep the cork and needle assembly floating near the center of the cup.

Floating Compass

1) Use a marker to write N, S, E, W on the cup, as shown.
2) Magnetize your needle (see next page).
3) Fill the cup with water and place it where it won't be jiggled.
4) Place a small piece of cork into the cup so it is floating in the center.
5) Carefully lay the magnetized needle on top of the cork.

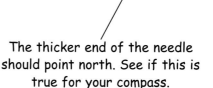

The thicker end of the needle should point north. See if this is true for your compass.

Magnetizing the Needle

Rub one end of the needle along a magnet. (Be careful! Needles are sharp!) Always rub in the same direction. Do this about 30 times to magnetize your needle. The more magnetized your needle is, the more accurate your compass will be. The larger the needle, the more magnetized it can be. Try different magnets and different-sized needles to find the best ones for your compass. Test the magnet's strength by picking up a pin or a paper clip.

Test Your Compass

Once you've built your compass, place it on a table and wait for the needle to come to rest. Now try moving the compass to a new place on the table. The needle should resettle and point north again. Try making all three compasses to see which one works best. (After a while, the needles will lose their magnetism, but they're easy to remagnetize.)

As long as you have a compass, you should be able to find your way.

Tip: Nearby metal objects may affect how your compass works.

INDEX OF SUPPLIES

1. Birdseed

2. Cardboard box

3. Clay plant pot bottom

4. Clear plastic cups

5. Cork (small piece)

6. Dish soap

7. Flat board

8. Helium-filled balloons

9. Lightbulb box

10. Magnet

11. Milk carton

12. Paper or Styrofoam cups

13. Paper towel roll

14. Pencil or pen

15. Pennies

16. Pie pan or baking tray

17. Plastic garbage bag

18. Plastic wrap

19. Screws and nails

20. Seeds or small plants

21. Sewing needle or pin

22. Shoe

23. Shoe box

24. Skewers

25. Soil

26. Stick

27. Straws

28. Tape

29. Thread

30. Wire coat hangers

31. Wooden dowel

32. Wooden post